# After dark

N.F

BookLeaf
Publishing
India | USA | UK

Presentation by *BookLeaf Publishing*

Web: www.bookleafpub.com

E-mail: info@bookleafpub.com

ISBN: 9789357447973

First edition 2022

# DEDICATION

To all the night owls.

# ACKNOWLEDGEMENT

Thank you to those, mostly my sister, who encouraged me to face this challenge of writing poems on a daily basis and who believed that I could accomplish to write for myself. Even though most of my family did not know about my poetry, I still want to thank them for having shown their support regardless of what I was doing in particular. So, a huge thank you and a big kiss on the forehead to my brother and his fiancé, my father and sister and many more. You mean the world to me. No sarcasm here.

A huge thank you to Bookleaf Publishing for presenting me with this opportunity.

Of course, a thank you to the people that inspired some of these poems, sometimes through mere interaction.

And lastly thank you reader, who spend their time with me and my words, who was willing to give me a chance at making you feel what I've felt or exploring your own emotions with me. It was a blast.

# The ocean we carry

Tears welled up in my eyes, as I read heartfelt words of death, love and betrayal. When I took my glasses off to wipe my eyes, there were little drops of salty water stuck to the lenses that reflected whole lifetimes in a single emotion.

-How beautiful to carry the ocean in oneself.

# The women that came before me

Sometimes being a woman frightens me. There are obvious reasons for that, but putting that aside, I fear not being able to live up to the women that came before me, who were brave enough to fight battles far beyond my knowledge, who climbed mountains so future generations could build houses on them.
But with time I've learned that I'm proud and honoured by my heritage, to have so many strong leaders to look up to, to share a history and a fight together. It gives me the chance to make them proud someday

# Labels

I always hated labels.
I understand that for some they are important to underline who they are and I will always have deep respect for them.
But do not be so naive to think you can put me into a box of your design, without me spending every second to escape that prison you so arrogantly build for your made-up version of me.

# Waffles in the woods

Lies sometimes are disguised like a stack of waffles with syrup dripping down their sides and a fresh piece of butter on top in the middle of the forest. The ones out of children's tales and movies.
Traps so obvious that we actively choose to look the other way and accept the promised trap in hopes to tase the sugary sweetness instead.

 -Sometimes the sugar coated lies are too tempting, but they remain lies
  nonetheless.

# Words to trust

Words are often used as a tool of manipulation,
so don't trust every I LOVE U that comes your
way.
The apple might look red and sweet, but be sure
it is not poisoned inside before taking a bite.
It might be honey dripping off their lips, but how
many bees will sting you, when you get close to
try and taste it.

-Be careful of words that trick you with their
promise of forever.

# Bruises

I wore you like a bruise.


A little bit proud for having fought a battle and come out not only alive, but with blood on my knuckles and victorious.

A little bit scared, for I have never been backed up in a corner like that, having to face anything you threw at me.

A little bit ashamed, for I have allowed you to touch my skin, letting you graze my smooth features, leaving me bleeding, beaten and cold, aching for a softer touch.

I wore you like a bruise...open and visible. For everyone to see, for I have grown and learned to make myself kind trough you.
  -you searched for a place to lay down and rest, but couldn't find it anywhere on my body.

# Home

I always thought of my home as the house I was
born and grew up in.
But places and buildings don't follow you
through life.
I've tried to search for a home in people, but
people like to redecorate and paint the walls.
Even the ones closest to you aren't always able
to keep the rain away, helping you stay dry.
I tried to find a home in the things I liked to do
most, but when depression knocked on my door,
claiming my new home theirs, I left that one
behind as too.
Maybe it is time to build a home within myself.
-        I wonder if I will find a place to reside
in permanently.

# Liquor on your lips

I know you can only kiss me when your lips
have touched bourbon a hundred times before
and your eyes are so tightly shut all you can see
are stars dancing on the inside of your lids.

You say it is against your religion.

I have given up trying to hold your hand while
walking in a busy park, still feeling the sting of a
whip when you pulled your fingers away from
mine.

You say someone might see and people talk.

You never introduced me to your mother, your
sister or any of your friends. They don't even
know what my name sounds like coming from
your mouth.

You say they wouldn't understand. Though they
certainly would like me.

You slowly poisoned me like the liquor in your
blood, before we ever could get close enough to

build ourselves an empire. Your doors just were
too tightly shut.

It's been long enough and I cannot wait any
longer for you to decide I'm enough to climb the
fences you build around yourself. I've already
spent too much time praying to gods I don't
believe in to change the way things are, so you
can love me openly.
I know it's hard, but sometimes the hardest
decisions are worth the pain.


  -It's not your fault having lived in a world full
of hate all your life, but it is time for you to heal
and time for me to go.

# Flowers

Imagine a world without flowers.
What would I pick for you if I wanted to
surprise you?
Which petals would I tear from their core in
order to decide whether you loved me or not?
What would I remember to be your favourite, if
not your favourite flower?
What would I make a crown out of in a kingdom
of our own?
What would I hold to my nose when I want to
feel just a little closer to spring?

But imagine this instead. Me holding a small
bouquet of wildflowers out to you. Enjoy their
smell, press them between the pages of an old
book and think of me when you put them in a
vase, pretending them to be as fresh as on the
first day I gave them to you.

# Parallels

That's the tragedy of parallels, even though they fit together perfectly, their paths are never to cross.

-Complimenting each other sometimes isn't enough.

# Sword

you fought wars when you were too young to understand.
You weren't born with a sword in your hand, someone put it there. Lay it down and redefine yourself.


 -You were a warrior first; it is time to be someone else.

# Potential

You are like a lit candle. You carry all the
potential of a raging wild fire in you, but are so
controlled, that you rarely burn at all.
So, climb out of your cage and burn a whole city
to the ground.

  -Don't waste your potential burning suavely all
the while.

# Favourites

I'm your favourite painting, that you refuse to
show to anyone, because you fear that if eyes
other than your own look upon it, it would lose
all its meaning, all its beauty.

I'm that particular shirt in your dresser that you
don't wear anymore because you once lent it to
me and now all it does is remind you of me.

I'm your favourite pencil, that you hardly ever
sharpen because you don't want to run out of
lead, making the use of it impossible.

I'm that song you don't want to listen to too
often, but end up putting it on repeat anyway,
thus running out of joy within a week or two.

I'm your favourite movie, ice cream flavour and
breakfast cereal, that you can
watch or eat over and over again, brining you
comfort.

And yet here you are trying to shove me in
darkest corners of your mind, desperately
wanting to forget me.

# Only what's best

You always say you don't know what women want, yet you speak louder than ever, claiming to know what's best for us.

Examples include:

1. Women want a steady relationship, as to not be lonely anymore.

2. We want a job, but nothing too demanding.

3. We want to marry at all costs, making all our wishes come true.

5. We definitely want children, for what is a childless woman?

Then when we finally have children, we do not want to get back to our jobs, we much rather stay home with the kids, spending our days cleaning, cooking and waiting for our husband to come home. Being happy and content like that for the rest of time.

But let me tell you little person, that you are mistaken, for we women are hungry wolfs and you with your lie poisoned mouth look like a roasted chicken at Christmas dinner. There will be nothing left of you by the time new years comes around.

# Wooden puppet

Casual you said. No strings attached. But at the end I was a wooden puppet, so entangled in strings I needed help to get out of all the knots, caught up in a play we got tired of performing. So instead of waiting for someone to rescue me I cut myself loose and went on to find a new story to tell.

There was no use to untie a mess that was hopelessly entwined, not wanting to be functioning once more.

# Doubt

I'm a doubter not a believer.
No matter what I attempt to do, I will always doubt.
I doubt my abilities, then move on to be certain that my project won't go anywhere, no one will ever be interested in it. It won't ever be good enough anyway.
I admire those who have enough magic in themselves to dare to dream of bigger things, as big as the clouds will carry them. For those, the world is a blank canvas, only waiting for their first bold stroke.
But who knows, maybe some of these magnificent people are doubters too, searching for some change in their back pockets, wondering if it will ever be enough to reach the sky.
And maybe the world is waiting for my bold stroke on the canvas too. And maybe I will start doubting less and start believing, that there is in fact a place, a community, a person where I will be celebrated for my creations.

# They will not bend for you

I love how flowers bloom, despite you calling them ugly or smelly. They just don't give a frickle frackle about your unfiltered opinion on their appearance, refusing to bend or wilt for someone that doesn't know the power it takes to sprout and bloom in the harshest of winds. They know someone will come along wanting to pluck them so badly, for they are the most mesmerising plant they've ever come across. And even if they don't come along, they are strong in knowing that nature has created them with all the intention of making them as they are, as they should be.

-That is what it's like to be powerful.

# One last time

Go on, break my heart once more. I want to feel it shatter one more time between your hands. I want to feel you close to me one last time.
And then I don't want to feel anything from you ever again.

- A necessary cleansing.

# Intention

I know it was never your intention to hurt other people, to hurt me or yourself.
But I understand that our inner demons not only turn against ourselves but against others too. But do remember the world is not painted red with blood, it often just seems that way. Wait until the sun sets and the moon covers everything in a silvery light. Tell me what you feel then.

# Hunters

She was an angel with skin of hot chocolate,
every bit as sweet. Her torso corset bound; her
thighs fitted in ivory straps. She looked every bit
holy with her wings soft against her back.
But such women have an army on the run,
shooting them down even in flight, making sure
arrows stick to them with the bloody cloth.
Women always had to be brave like that.
Fly away, do not hide in hopes of staying
undiscovered.
What a waste it would be to never soar, bound to
the ground, wishing that the earth swallows us
whole.
There will be scars. Do not worry, I will tend to
your wounds, keep you with me until the time is
right for you to be send off when the next wind
comes knocking on the door.

  -You are too majestic not to fly.

# Her

Once in art class, the instructor told us to sketch something we liked. He looked at the finished pieces and asked me whether I liked people for choosing the girl across the room.
But I simply loved art and how could she be described any differently.